DON'T WORRY, MURRAY!

An Hachette UK Company
www.hachette.co.uk

Vie Books, an imprint of Summersdale Publishers Ltd
Part of Octopus Publishing Group Limited
Carmelite House
50 Victoria Embankment
LONDON
EC4Y 0DZ
UK

www.summersdale.com

Printed and bound in China

ISBN: 978-1-80007-015-8

Substantial discounts on bulk quantities of Summersdale books are available to corporations, professional associations and other organizations. For details contact general enquiries: telephone: +44 (0) 1243 771107 or email: enquiries@summersdale.com.

DON'T WORRY, MURRAY!

A Child's Guide to Help Overcome Worries

A My Healthy Mind Book

Anna Adams

vie

Josiane Vlitos

Murray had a **big** worry.

"I'M WORRIED,"
said Murray.

"What's your worry,
Murray?" asked Hoots.

"I'm worried about going to
my new school," he sniffed.
"It's big and noisy and
I might get lost."

4

"That's three worries. What are you going to do?" asked Hoots.

"I'm going to hide under my duvet until the worries go away," said Murray.

"I wouldn't do that," said Hoots, "when you hide from a worry, it will get **BIGGER**."

"Oh dear. I don't want that to happen," said Murray.

Murray started to
SHAKE
and feel a bit unwell.

"I think the worry has taken over my body."

"That's a normal way to feel when you're worried. I can help you," replied Hoots.

6

"You need to go over the
WORRY HILL
for your fears to disappear,"
said Hoots.

"Where is the Worry Hill?
Will you take me there?"
asked Murray.

"YES, but not yet,"
replied Hoots.

"Why not?"

"You still have
your pyjamas on!"

Murray and Hoots reached the
WORRY HILL.

"Oh dear," said Murray.
His tummy felt all
FLUTTERY.

"It's OK, Murray,
I'm with you,"
said Hoots.

THE WORRY HILL

"There are signposts to help you break down your worry.

Here's the first one!" said Hoots.

Imagine meeting smiley new friends

Murray closed his eyes and imagined **friendly faces** and a **lovely park** that they were all playing in.

He began to **SMILE**, but he quickly opened his eyes again.

"How was that, Murray?" asked Hoots.

"That was **fun**," Murray said,
"but now I'm even **more** worried.
What if I don't make any friends?"

"Of course you will! You're
a **good friend** to me
and others will want to be
friends with you too,"
comforted Hoots.

"Let's keep going up the hill,
Murray!"

"Come on," said Hoots,
"here's the next signpost."

"What does
that mean?"
asked Murray.

Find
your
battle
cry

"It means that you need to
CALL OUT LOUD
to help you feel **brave** enough to
beat your worry."

11

"Arrrrrggggggghhhwoooo!"

Murray cried, and the noise echoed around him.

"**Not quite,**" said Hoots. "It needs to be something that makes you feel **strong**, like '**I CAN DO THIS!**'"

"OK, I can do this." squeaked Murray.

"Let's do it together!"
Hoots exclaimed.

"I can do this!"

"WOW!" said Murray, "I'm starting to believe I really CAN do this! Oh, hang on, no, I'm STILL really worried. Can we just turn back and go home?"

"Let's just get to the next signpost, Murray, you're doing really well. I believe in you!" said Hoots.

"You do?" asked Murray.

"OF COURSE! Come on!"

IS IT FACT OR

FEELINGS?

"What does that mean?" said Murray.

"What are you thinking about when you feel worried?" asked Hoots.

"I'm thinking that the school is too big and I'll get lost. I might look silly, and no one will like me!" cried Murray.

"Are these thoughts FACTS, or do you think they are FEELINGS?" asked Hoots.

MURRAY SHRUGGED.

15

"Was the school too **big**?"

"No, it was **nice**."

"Did you get **lost**?"

"Umm, no, because there were people to ask if I didn't know where to go."

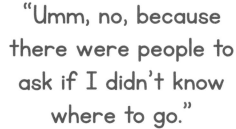

"Were the people nice?"

"Yes, the ones I met were really **friendly**."

"And, did they think you were **silly?**"

"No, they said they liked my backpack and we played in the playground."

"There you are! Your worry is based on **feelings** rather than **facts!**"

"Yes!"

"It is?"

17

"But what if it's all different this time?" asked Murray.

"That's just your worry trying to **TRIP YOU UP,**" said Hoots.

"**LOOK,** Murray! We're almost at the top of the **WORRY HILL.**"

"Here's the next signpost," said Hoots.

TALK TO YOUR WORRY.

"What do you want to say
to your worry, Murray?"

19

"Worry, what will happen if I go to school?" asked Murray.

The cloud GRUMBLED overhead, like it was CRUNCHING on his words. Murray hid behind Hoots.

The worry talked back with a deep voice,

" What's the WORST that could happen? "

"OH NO!"
said Murray.

"Come on," called Hoots, "you can do it!"

"I might get lost. I might not make a friend. I might look silly!" said Murray.

The worry grumbled again, then said,

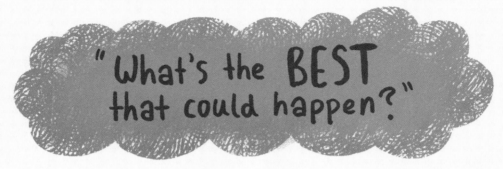

"What's the BEST that could happen?"

"I find my way round to my class, I make new friends to play with, and I feel happy." Murray smiled. He liked this idea.

"What's most LIKELY to happen?"

"I get lost on my way to my class," said Murray.

"What will you do then?" asked Hoots.

"I'll ask someone in my new class or look for signs!" said Murray.

"What about
making friends?"
asked Hoots.

"And what about
looking silly?"
Hoots added.

"I will talk to the people
I met when I looked round,"
said Murray.

"I won't look silly,
because...", and here
Murray took a DEEP
BREATH and said,

"I CAN DO THIS!"

The worry let out an almighty

P O P

and disappeared.

Suddenly, the birds began to
sing and the sun came out.

23

"Murray, you've done it!"

"*I have? I HAVE!*"

Murray jumped **UP** and **DOWN**
and they started to race down the
other side of the hill.

"I can see the school from here!"
shouted Murray.

24

"Yes, do you still
feel worried, Murray?"

"A little bit,"
said Murray.

"In that case, let's
see what the **next
signpost** says,"
replied Hoots.

Instead of a signpost, they found a mailbox
with a rolled-up piece of paper inside.

Hoots unrolled the paper. It said
"MURRAY'S WORRY-BUSTING PLAN"
at the top, and underneath were all the steps
that they had found on the Worry Hill.

Murray's Worry-Busting Plan

- Imagine meeting smiley new friends.
- Find your **battle cry**.
- Ask yourself: is it **fact** or **feelings**?
- **Talk** to your worry.
- What's the **worst** that could happen?
- What's the **best** that could happen?
- What's **most likely** happen?
- And don't forget to **squeeze your nose!**

"What does that last bit mean?" said Murray.

"Oh, that's the best bit!" said Hoots. "If you need to feel better, try some squeezy breathing!"

"How do I do that?" asked Murray.

1. "First, squish down your right nostril."

2. "Take a deep breath in through the left nostril."

3. "Now swap paws and squish down your left nostril."

4. "Then breathe out through your right nostril."

Murray tried it and made
funny **SQUEAKY** noises
with his nose.

"I have a nose-trumpet!"

"And how do you feel now?"
asked Hoots.

"I FEEL GOOD!"
answered Murray.
My worry is about the size
of a grain of sand. No, I think
it's even smaller!"

"You have safely
crossed the Worry
Hill, Murray!"

30

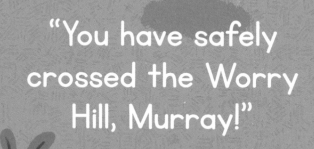

"Are you ready to go
to school now?" asked Hoots.

"YES, I AM! Today is going
to be a REALLY GOOD DAY!"
said Murray, and off he
ran to school.

Have you enjoyed reading this book with your child?
If so, why not write a review on your favourite website?

If you're interested in finding out more about our books,
find us on Facebook at **Summersdale Publishers**,
on Twitter at **@Summersdale** and
on Instagram at **@summersdalebooks**
and get in touch. We'd love to hear from you!

Thanks very much for buying this Summersdale book.
www.summersdale.com